The Siege of King's Lynn
1643

Including the first reprinting for 350 years of

'A briefe and true Relation of the Siege and Surrendering of Kings Lyn to the Earle of Manchester'

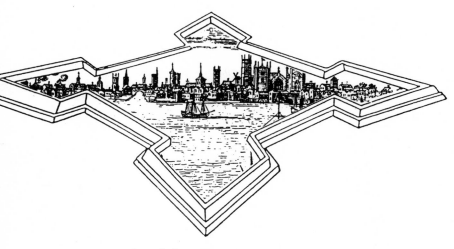

Edited by Susan Yaxley

The Larks Press

First 1,000 copies printed and published by
The Larks Press
Ordnance Farmhouse, Guist Bottom, Dereham
Norfolk NR20 5PF

June 1993

Reprinted September 1996

British Library Cataloguing-in-Publication Data
A catalogue record for this book is available from the British Library

ISBN 0 948400 20 X

♻ Before the Siege ♻

It is now 350 years since the port of Lynn Regis was besieged by Parliamentarian troops in the early years of the Civil War. Lynn was then the most desirable port of entry to the eastern counties of England, a place of considerable strategic importance, supplier of ten counties with essential commodities and the outlet for the area's chief marketable crop, corn.

Lynn had grown prosperous as Wisbech and Boston declined. It had become the chief seaport for Northampton, Cambridge, Leicester, Oakham, Bury St. Edmunds and Sleaford, and supplied these places with coal, salt and fish. It was also increasingly sending supplies to London by the coastal route. On the quayside at Lynn might be seen fishing vessels which sailed to Iceland and the Baltic, colliers from Newcastle, ships with cargoes from Elbing, Hamburg, Amsterdam, and Antwerp. The buildings of the town were huddled close to the water-front and the market-places which together were the hub of Lynn's daily life. The town's defences on the other hand, the walls, gates and ditches faced resolutely to the south and east and towards the sea whence, at various times, the townspeople had feared invasion by the French, or the Spanish or the predatory pirates from Dunkirk.

The governors of Lynn, the common councillors, aldermen and mayor, were drawn from the class of wealthy men who dominated the life of the town. These were the brewers, lawyers and ship-owning merchants many of whom had large establishments near the water-front with extensive warehouses and watergates. For these men, in normal times, trade took precedence over national politics; but the disturbed early years of the Long Parliament were far from normal. Who could say, in 1642, which would most benefit the trade of Lynn, a victory for Parliament or for the King? Peace, undoubtedly, would be preferable to either, and like many another corporation at this time Lynn hedged its bets and prayed for a reconciliation between the factions. Men of all opinions, however, were agreed that the defences of Lynn must be strengthened and its powder supplies refurbished. At the beginning of 1642 we find the Council ordering that six barrels of gunpowder were to be stored at the Market Cross, three at St. Ann's Fort, four at Trinity Hall and five at St. Margaret's Mount. More hazardously it was agreed that every citizen might purchase 2 or 3 lbs of powder at 14d per pound, 'to keepe in his howse ready for the comon defence'. Alehouse-keepers were ordered to inform the aldermen if any stranger lodged with them for more than one night. There is no mention of the nature of the expected enemy, but it is quite clear which way the political wind was blowing in the Council. Alderman Doughty, accused in September by Sir Edmund Mundford of being a 'great opposer of orders of Parliament', felt it necessary to protest his innocence and have it recorded in the Hall Book that he was 'more than ordinary forward in his obedyence to orders of Parlyament'.

The Parliamentarians seem to have been firmly in the saddle at the outbreak of hostilities in August 1642. The two M.P.s, John Percival and Thomas Toll were active in London getting Parliamentary authority for the fortifying of Lynn, and in October Mr Toll brought direct orders that the town should 'muster and trayne' its trained bands, fortify the town and put in custody any who sent money, plate or munitions to the King to enable him to wage 'a wicked and unnaturall warre against his Majesties good subjects'. On the same day the Council ordered that £100 should be sent to Parliament. At the same time, Hillen claims, money and plate to a similar value was sent by the townsmen to the King in

Oxford. With hindsight we may suspect that some of the council had supported this action.

During the anxious period following the indecisive battle of Edgehill, King's Lynn continued to fortify. Drawbridges were planned at the South and East gates: twenty barrels of gunpowder were purchased; Captains Slaney and Atkins trained the unwarlike people of Lynn. Early in December both M.P.s and Town Clerk Leake (a covert royalist) were summoned by the Deputy-Lieutenants to a meeting in Norwich to discuss county strategy in the event of the arrival of 'forreign forces much feared to be sodainly landed on some part of the coaste of Norfolk, Suffolk & Essex'. Their fears, doubtless, were of mercenaries enlisted by the Queen landing at Lynn or elsewhere in support of the King.

The real danger to Lynn, however, did not come from the sea, but from the countryside surrounding the town where a number of royalist gentry were quietly gathering their strength. Chief amongst these were the Lestranges of Hunstanton, who were able to call on the support of imposing ranks of friends and relations, the Mordaunts of Massingham, the Hovells of Hillington, the Spelmans of Congham, the Yelvertons of Rougham and the Pastons of Appleton. There were in fact few gentry in this area likely to oppose them. The Lestranges had already been marked down as 'malignants' by the Parliamentarians for their refusal to contribute to levies, and orders for them to be arrested and disarmed had been issued in both October and December of 1642, but without effect. During the early spring of 1643 it seems that Sir Hamon and his sons used their personal popularity, plus an offer of £1,000 towards the fortifying of Lynn, to activate the royalists in the town. In March there were disturbances coinciding with the abortive royalist rising at Lowestoft. Colonel Oliver Cromwell, having nipped the Lowestoft trouble in the bud, sped back to Lynn 'because the Malevolents began to raise combustions there'.

On May 5th, the worried councillors sent a letter to Miles Corbet at the Parliamentary Committee of Informations seeking authority 'to examine all such persons and strangers as now are lately or hereafter shall shroud themselves within this town which may be supposed to be Malignants...and to remove or apprehend such as Mr Mayor ... shall think meet'. On May 8th orders were issued to the Mayor and Justices of Lynn to apprehend Sir Hamon Lestrange, his sons Nicholas and Roger, his grandson Nicholas, and his brother-in-law Sir Charles Mordaunt. A further eight royalist gentlemen were named, some of whom had come some distance to lend their support to the Lynn rebellion. Whether from sympathy with their activities, inability to capture them, or from fear of the local effect of such an arrest, the Mayor failed to carry out this order and the royalist faction continued to grow. In July 1643 we hear from the news-sheets of a riot involving 200 royalists. We also learn from Lady Lestrange's accounts that her husband found it necessary to go into hiding at this time, spending £5 5s. 'when he travailed to avoyd the Troopers'. Truly a gentleman whatever the circumstances, Sir Hamon also laid out at this time for '3 payre of spectacles 18d, and for a tortois shell case for them 4s., for a looking glasse and making a case to it 11s., for a payre of sizers, beard irons & bodkin to the case 5s. and for Dammasking of them 11s.'.

The main royalist forces under the Earl of Newcastle, meanwhile, were fast approaching the eastern counties from the north. Early in August they succeeded in taking Gainsborough. Most of Lincolnshire fell quickly into their hands and near panic seized the Committee of the Eastern Association sitting at Cambridge. 'It's no longer disputing' wrote Cromwell to them, 'but Out instantly all you can!' In Lynn even the loyalty of the trained bands could no longer be relied upon, for the royalist attorney, Walter Kirby, had managed to get himself appointed one of the captains. On August 6th the remaining Parliamentarian councillors met to discuss the crisis. The Hall Book records that 'Whereas in these dangerous times it is informed to this house that not only a great companye of strangers are now come into this burghe, but that an over multitude of such strangers will suddenly pester this said Burgh, it is therefore ordered...that generall and spetiall notis shal be given to all & every the householders & inhabitants of this burgh that henceforth they receive not nor presume to entertaine into ther houses any person or persons whatsoever before first they acquaint Mr Maior...' But to which side did the Mayor owe his allegiance? This question was decisively answered on August 13th when Gurlin became a mouthpiece for the royalists, ordered the arrest of the pro-Parliamentarian councillors and the detention in their houses of the M.P.s Percival and Toll, directed the town's ordnance towards the land rather than the sea, and declared Sir Hamon Lestrange 'Governor of Lynn' in the King's name.

Sir Hamon Lestrange was sixty years old and already a grandfather. He was fond of books and music, a man of aristocratic temperament who was a natural royalist accustomed to living in the grand manner. His two elder sons, Nicholas and Hamon, were married and had children. Roger, the youngest son, had been at Grey's Inn running up considerable debts for his father to pay, until, in 1639, he dashed up to Scotland to have his share of the action in the Bishops' War. He found this a disillusioning experience, but it did not lessen his appetite for military adventure.

Sir Hamon and his wife employed at least 18 servants at Hunstanton Hall, including a falconer and a fool, and their expenses amounted to over £2,500 per year. Luxury items in their accounts, family coach repairs, expensive medicines and black marble for their stable floor, seem to indicate a lavish life-style for the period. Even more interestingly, the accounts show that they could not finance this life-style without regular borrowing. Sir Hamon had annual loans of about £1,000, borrowed, often from his female relatives, at 4% interest. A civil war in which Norfolk was dominated by his political enemies might well mean that the Lestranges faced financial disaster.

The news that Lynn had declared for the King caused alarm amongst the Parliamentarian forces. A detachment of troops from Essex, under Captain William Poe, was immediately despatched to establish a blockade and control the bridges and roads leading to the town. The Earl of Manchester and Colonel Cromwell moved quickly to set up mortars on the west bank of the Ouse facing Lynn's water-front. The royalist gentry seem to have behaved with considerable bravado in the early days, attempting to ambush Poe and his men and to capture '3 or 400 beefs' bound for Setchey market. They set fire to trees outside the walls of the town and to the almshouses at Gaywood which might have given shelter to the besiegers, and also destroyed some houses near the South gate which apparently hindered the operations of the defenders. Captain Poe, in a letter to his Essex Committee, said the royalists had threatened to cut him and his troops 'as small as herbs to the pot', but gave his opinion that they were but 'cowardly cavaliers'.

A regular bombardment of the town was kept up, apparently causing great terror amongst the essentially peaceable inhabitants. On Sunday, September 3rd, according to an unidentified letter quoted by the nineteenth-century historian of Lynn, Richards, 'in the middle of the sermon, came a shot of 18 lbs. weight in at the window over the west door of St. Margaret's church, and took the middle pillar a great part off and broke it in many hundred pieces, dispersing them in all directions all over the church. One piece of the stone fell into a seat at the lower end of the church where five men sat, split the board before them, on which they laid their books; but no harm was done to them. The preacher, a reverend divine named Mr Hinson, left his sermon and came out of the church, and all the people departed in a most confused manner, some leaving their hatts, some their books, and some their scarves; but, praised be God, no further hurt was done to any person.'

The Earl of Manchester, meanwhile, from his headquarters at Setchey, did his best to organise an army fit to mount an assault upon Lynn. Initially the Eastern Association Committee thought 2,000 troops would be sufficient, three quarters of these to be raised from Norfolk, Suffolk and Essex, and the rest from the other eastern counties. Quality, however, proved more important than quantity, and the Earl complained that he was too often sent men with 'no arms, no clothes, no colours, no drums' who were all too likely to desert before ever engaging in battle. However, by September 7th his force was within musket-shot of the town, they had blockaded the southern and eastern approaches to Lynn and cut off its fresh water supplies from the Gaywood River to the north. Though summoned three times to surrender, the royalist garrison remained apparently defiant. One of their replies had twenty-five signatures attached including those of Recorder Parlett, the newly-elected Mayor, Edmund Hudson, and Sir Hamon himself. 'We send our names' they wrote, 'lest you should forget to plunder us when you have taken our town'.

The royalists' will to resist, nevertheless, must have been ebbing away with every day that they failed to receive news of assistance from the King's army in Lincolnshire. Charles I, at this stage, made a crucial decision to concentrate his efforts on the reduction of Gloucester, and Newcastle feared to move further south while Hull remained in Parliamentarian hands. Outside the walls of Lynn everything appeared to be in readiness: boats for a river assault, ladders for scaling the walls, an army which by this date may have been as many as 8,000. The Earl of Manchester advised the people of Lynn to send away their women and children and let it be known that Saturday 16th of September was the day set for a final assault.   At the eleventh hour Sir Hamon Lestrange agreed to negotiate the surrender of the town.

Less Puritan than Yarmouth or Norwich, and more exposed to the influence of local cavaliers, Lynn had allowed itself to become the 'last chance saloon' of the Norfolk royalists. Those in the town who transferred their allegiance to the King had gambled Lynn's wealth on the fortunes of war and lost.

Virtually all that is known of the surrender and the events immediately following is contained in the contemporary pamphlet which is here reprinted for the first time since that eventful year.

Norfolk Museums Service, King's Lynn Museum.
Part of Lynn's water-front from an 18th century engraving (Saylmaker)

A briefe and true

RELATION

of the

Siege and Surrendering of Kings Lyn
To the Earle of

MANCHESTER

Kings Lyn is seated upon an arme of the sea which washes one side of it, it hath surrounding the other side, one small part excepted, a large water fed from the aforesaid arme; its of an indifferent height, the parts about being commanded by it, being rich Marshes, through which passeth at the tides the salt water: It had been for a good while cunningly Fortifying it selfe under pretence of Neutrality, and when at any time the Parliament upon their miscariages questioned them, or required any thing to be done by them, they still refused, and by degrees appeared more and more for the other party against the Parliament: The Earle of Manchester being made Major Generall of the Associated Counties, thought most necessary to secure that back-doore, which being so convenient an inlet to the enemy, might divert him when he should advance with his powers towards the North, for the freeing of Lincolneshire and other parts from the miseries they suffer by the enemy: it was much disputed whether it were not better to proceed by blocking it up, rather then to take it by force; the Towne being of that strength that no ordinary power could take it, had they that which was fit for defence, but it was at last resolved to attempt it by force, and for that purpose it was thought good to seize the Towne of old Lyn, which is in Marshland, which by a party of my Lords Forces was accordingly done, and Ordnance planted, which kept the Towne in continuall Alarmes, and did so terrifie the people with their shot and Granadoes, that they durst hardly abide in any of their houses that were towards that side, the shot flying daily into the houses in the Tuesday market place, and other places, the Towne was approched in severall other places, two of which were on the side next to the mote, the one by the Causey that leades to the South, the other to the East gate: The enemy at the first sallied out with much courage, especially from the East gate and at once fired two houses in Gauwood, intending to have done so to the whole Towne, that our forces might not Quarter in there, but the party that sallied out was well beaten, and the rest of the towne preserved, though the inhabitants were not worthy of such a favour, who fled all away upon the approach of our Forces; all things being put in order we called in pioneers from all parts round, and fell to breaking ground, and by degrees had brought our approaches within halfe Musket shot, yet were we little the neerer the gaining the towne thereby, onely the better inabledto batter their walls, gates and Forts; a little before the towne was yeilded we discovered a hill of firme ground that was neerer to that end of the towne next the sea, which we had begun to forme into a battery, which would have so annoyed them, that they would not have knowne where to have been secure, and by which a breach might have been made; but this also gave us no great hopes of entrance, they making up as fast, as we should have beaten downe, therefore we resolved upon storming the towne Saturday morning, and to that purpose had called in many Boats, with which we intended to attache it by water, and many cart loads of Ladders, which we intended for the land side: during this hot service we lost about four men, one a Canoneer, who was shot through the side with a drake bullet, he was not dead when the Towne was taken, but it was no likelyhood but he would, he was a good Canoneer, and a man right to his party, we had one shot with a bullet through the shoulder, neere the necke: and one Lieutenant had his arme shot off, on which he died suddenly after, it was with a Cannon shot through a Port-hole, so skilfull were they, that they would shoot three times together into one Port-hole: In this violent playing with Cannon and small shot we beleeve above eighty lost their lives on both sides, which is the rather added, because people enquire usually how many were killed, as if they loved to heare of killing of men; and also to rectifie the Judgements of men, who will be apt to credit a story of three, four or five thousand men slaine at such a Siege, and such a siege; its true, storming and entring breaches usually wast men, but we were not come to this; when it was resolved and declared on Saturday morning to storme, we

A Medal of the Earl of Manchester

hapily received a letter the Friday morning, importing a willing-nesse in the Towne to capitulate, which they said, and its like truly, they did not send as fearing the taking the Town, but to avoid the effusion of blood: My Lord having before advised them to send their women and children out of the Towne; which he did for the same reason: This Treaty was accepted, and eight persons for the Towne, and eight for my Lord appointed to Treat at Gau-wood at the Quarter of that valiant and pious Scot Serjeant Major

Hoames, and to begin at five of the clock on Friday night, which being done, order was given upon paine of death, that none should shoot a shot, or worke upon their Works during the time of the Treaty; which was inviolably kept on my Lords part.

The Commissioners for my Lord Manchester, were Sir John Pagrave, Colonell Russell, Colonell Walton, Master Philip Calthrop, Master John Pickering, Master Gregory Gosset, Master John Spilman, and Master William Good.

Those for the Towne, were Sir Hammon le Strange, Sir Richard Hovill, Master Clinch, Master Dearham, Master Pallet Recorder, Master Hudson, the Mayor elect; Master Leeke, and Master Kerbio; when they were come, they had no power to treat, nor to determine, which being demanded the reason of, they answered, that they intended onely to draw things to a head, and to have them ratified by the Mayor at a Common-Hall; as for a Commission from his Majestie, inabling any to be Governour, or to fortifie the Towne, there was none produced, it was beleeved one of the Commissioners had one, but he did not shew it; there was therefore a dispatch made to the Mayor, who gave it them.

The Demands of these Gentlemen was to this effect; That in regard the Towne of Kings Lyn had a government by Charter, from the Kings of England, and was not an offender in any thing, they therefore desired to be left in their former state, onely fortifications demolished, and to have free egresse and regresse as formerly: They desired also, that all houses, lands and estates, be left to pay taxes by distresse, onely where it was to be had, and persons of men to be free, that the ships, goods, and personall estates taken to be restored, or satisfaction: that all strangers come into the towne, be set at liberty, that the aspersion of Delinquencie or Malignancie be abolished, and that the Earle of Manchester grant Protections to them that desire them. My Lord Manchesters Commissioners replied, That they had offended, for they had not paid in the second part of the 400000 pounds, they have made no assessement of the fifth, and twentieth part, nor sent in horse; and on the contrary, refused to send up Delinquents sent for by the Parliament, pretended to hold the towne for King and Parliament, and yet refuse to deliver the towne, or give enterance to the Earle, who demands it for King and Parliament; and have received the dis-affected into the towne, and dis-armed the well-affected; imprisoned Members of the House of Commons, and some of the Committee, they have imployed armes intrusted with them for the Association against them; money gathered for the service of the Parliament, they have made use of to defend the towne against the Parliament and Association, and many of the goods of the well-affected they have taken and imployed for the defence of the

On the two following pages:

Map of King's Lynn made by Henry Bell in 1692

Key:

1. St. Margarets Church   2. St. Nicholas Church
4. White Friers   6. All Saints Church   7. St. James Church
8. St. Georges Hall   9. The Towne Hall   10. East gate
11. South gate   12. Ladies Mount   13. Almes Houses
15. Tuesday Market place   17. The Glas house   18. Corne mill
19. An Oyle mill   20. Worlds end   21. Fish ponds
22. Kings Stathyard   23. Common Stathyard   24. Purflett Bridge
25. St. Anns Fort   26. Gray Friers   27. Augustine Friers
28. Black Friers   29. North Ferry   30. South Ferry

THE GROUND PLAT
KINGS L

15 Tusday Market place
17 The Glashouse
18 Go   mill
19 An Oyle mill
20 Worlds end
21 Fisk ponds
22 Kings   Stathyard
23 Common
24 Purflett Bridge
25 S. Anns Fort

8 S. Georges
9 The Towne   Hall
10 East   gate
11 Saethic
12 Ladies Mount
13 Almes Houses

Scale of common paces

100   200   300   400   500   600   700   800

THE   R

4 White
26 Gray
27 Augustine
28 Black
29 North
30 South

11

26

RIVER OVSE

old Lyn

towne; therefore they appeared to be great offenders: Yet to prevent effusion of bloud, if they will deliver the towne by Saturday
nine in the morning, they shall have priviledge and freedome; as
for freedome from Ordinances of Parliament, they must expect
no such thing; as for satisfaction, their defection hath beene the
cause of all their sufferings, and so cannot be satisfied, but the
contrary is expected & required, not onely for the former, but
also for the time spent in reducing to obedience the town, & a
moneths pay to the souldiers; for their persons & estates, they shall
not be molested for any thing done since the Earls coming; but
for Horse and Arms that were in the town they must be delivered
to the Earl at his entrance.

After much debate upon the Particulars, which held from seven
at night until eight the next night, a dinner time onely excepted, it was agreed in substance as followes:

*First, That Kings Lyn with the Ordnance, Armes and Ammunition
in the Towne, be delivered to the Earle, and the Earle to enter the
Town.*

*Secondly, That the Gentlemen strangers in the Towne should have
liberty to depart with every man a Horse, Sword, and Pistols.*

*Thirdly, That the Townesmen shall enjoy all undoubted Rites and
Priviledges appertaining to them, with free trading to their advantage,
so far as may consist with Law.*

*Fourthly, That all Prisoners on both sides be restored and set at lib-
erty.*

*Fiftly, That the Earles Commissioners shall signifie to the Parliament,
and to the Earle of Warwick, the desire of the towne of Lyn, con-
cerning the ships taken by the Parliaments ships, and to that they can
give no other answer.*

Sixtly, That neither the person nor estates of any Inhabitants, Gentry, or Strangers, now residing in Lyn, shall be hereafter molested for any thing past, or done by them, since the Earle of Manchesters comming into these parts.

Seventhly, That for preventing of plundering, ten shillings a man be raised for all foot souldiers under the Earles Command, and a fortnights pay for all Officers under the degree of a Captaine, and this is to be levied upon the Towne.

Eightly, That Sir Hammon le Strange, Sir Richard Hovill, Captaine Clinch, Master Recorder, Master Dearing, and Master William Leeke, be left as Hostages untill Conditions be performed agreed upon.

That which is observable during this Treaty, is, that the Towne, or rather the unrulie souldiers shot at our men, contrary to accord, and fell to work upon their workes, and as it is conceived, with intent to cut ditches at the spring-tides, to drowne our workes, which we discovering, made use of, to hold them up to our termes, otherwayes they were all prisoners, if we stood upon it. This agreement being carryed to the Mayor and Aldermen, &c. there were some explainary exceptions, as that it was not exprest in the pre-amble, that the Towne be delivered for King and Parliament; that somewhat was not exprest in favour or vindication of the Mayor, that any should be exempt from bearing part of that raised to content the souldiers, or to that effect, which my Lord by a Letter, or short Declaration satisfied them in, and then one of their Commissioners returned with the last and full resolution, that the Gates should be opened, and we enter: During this latter businesse, we mistrusting they would faulter, we drew all our horse and foote into meadowes, which we put into such a

posture as might be most terrible to the enemy, making a large
front, when God knowes what depths they stood, then beating
the Drums, and sounding the Trumpets, as if we had been pre-
sently to march into the Towne: Col: Russell, that noble and
valiant Gentleman had the Van, and Col: Walton the Reere: Colonell Russell marched on foot towards the East-gate, when he
came within Musquet shot, the Commissioner that was imployed
to make way came backe, and told the Colonell, that the season
of the night would not permit to open the great Gate, they must
therefore be content to march one by one at the Wicket, if any
shall question our discretion in entring in at a Wicket, and at
twelve a clock at night, let them know, that we did not know
what alterations might be by morning, nor how the ruder part
might take courage and deny us entrance; we thought it best therefore to take the present time, besides our men were the next morning to have stormed it, otherway the spring-tide would have
spoiled us; but when the Wicket was open, and we going to enter,
the Commissioner againe returned, and told us there was a rude
multitude of about forty or fifty, that swore none should enter
there, and if any did, they would be the death of them, which
they might have made good to five hundred, if we had stood to
it: they had there a parley of neere two houres, some saying Articles must be performed: others, that they would not condescend
nor obey, nor should the Mayor and Commissioners acts binde
them, Crying shoote, shoote, and one Canoneere they turned out,
because he would not give fire upon us, as himselfe said: at last
one of them cryed, give fire, which being in the dead of the night,
made some of the forward Countreymen and others on horse
backe, who rid by the side of the foote that marched, to fall off
their horses, and some into the ditch, so terrible was the word,

The correct position for the musketeer on the command 'Give fire!'
Redrawn from Hexham's 'Principles of the Art Militarie'

Give fire: but at last this multitude was pacified and departed, which to speake truth was from heaven, for had they continued obstinate, wee could not have gained the towne: they disperst, the Colonell entred, and his souldiers, who marched to their quarters at the South-gate according to order; in our passage through the towne, not one man appeared, only the women, who for the generall cryed, God blesse us, whether for fear or love, you may guesse. Thus being possest of the Towne, and having drawne a party into the Tuesday market place both of horse and foote, and set strong watches at every place, the Mayor came to the Colonell, of whom we demanded why the Armes of the Towne, according to the agreement was not brought into the market place, he re-plyed, that the season of the night would not permit, but in the morning it should be done, which satisfied the Colonell, for we saw they were perfectly subdued, and their spirits as to opposition quite gone. If it shall be further enquired, why, or what should be the reason this towne of so great strength should yeeld to so small a power; it is answered, first the inhabitants were such as had not been accustomed to war, and were much frighted by the Granadoes, though to speake truth, there was some defect in them, so that they did little, only falling among a timerous people. Secondly, they had no souldiers, but inhabitants, and of them not many fighters; but chiefely for this reason, they knew my Lord was noble, made up of love and meeknesse, that conditions would be performed, their trade and markets open, a garrison would spend money among them, and if they held out, they should it was like lose many of their lives, and be blockt up by sea and land, if not taken, and their estates at last become a prey to the conquerour: there is one other question, or rather an exception to be answered, which as we understood in the Army, was that the Londoners tooke exceptions that my Lord sate downe before the Towne; For answer to this, though it be a sad thing that accounts must be given to those that understand not the affaires of War, nor whom it so much concerned as the associated Counties, yet thus much may be said, my Lord thought action would have pleased them, because they complaine so for want of action, and besides to reduce a towne to obedience that they traded with, and the holding out of it so much prejudice to them, should rather have put them upon his encouragement, then finding fault: Besides he hopes shortly to be in Lincolnshire, and to drive the enemy out thence, which he could not have done, that towne not secured, and if God prosper his honour as well there, as in this late action, he shall cleare the Countries, make way for the Londoners increase of trade and accommodation with provisions for the City,

Lincolnshire being one of their best magazines for the belly.

We thus possest of the Towne: the next morning about nine of the clock his Lordship marched from his head quarter, with his life-guard, a brave Troope commanded by that valiant Gentleman Captaine Rich, and divers Knights and Gentlemen being come into the Towne, he repaired to the Sermon, where one of his Chaplaines preached, to give God thankes for his happy and peaceable entry, the Ministers both in fore and afternoone bending their discourses that way, and indeed God was seen exceedingly in the businesse, and so much the more as the arme of flesh was weak, they laboured also to possesse the people of a blessing to them, and to that purpose gave many cleer instances, too large to be here inserted, whether the people thought so or not did not appear, but they will suddenly finde it so; my Lord hath his Quarter at Alderman Tolls a Member of the House of Commons, who was so roughly dealt with, in the time of the Siege, that he was constrained to make an escape out at a window into the arme of the sea, his house being guarded in all parts else by Musketiers; many others returned that had fled out of the Towne, who were hapily again possest of their dwellings, though with great diminution of their estates, which to repaire, it were good forme course were taken, for there is nothing more reasonable, then that those that forsake all for the Cause, should be satisfied in point of dammage; Colonell Walton hath for the present the Government of the towne; thus we see how providence orders, he that was lately lockt up for three daies and three nights at Oxford in a poor chamber without food, is now Governour of as great and strong a towne as Oxford; in which service he will doubtlesse behave himselfe so well that the towne shall not have cause to complaine, and will be able to say that at the delivery of his charge, which was said by Master Ash at the evening sermon after the entring the towne, that he was confident notwithstanding the entrance was in the dead of the night, yet a halfepenny worth of wrong had not been done to any in the towne. The first resolution taken for the better and more orderly government of the Souldiers, and content of the people was to have every morning at eight a clocke a Sermon, which was to be performed by the Ministers of the Towne, and my Lords Chaplaines, which will undoubtedly keepe a good Harmony betweene them: And thus briefely you have the most materiall passages past in the Service; the next thing to be done is the dismissing the Gentlemen Strangers, seizing of Armes, and what by Articles was to be delivered, setling the Garrison, that so the place being secured his Lordship may advance,

Take one observation more, the Towne of Lyn may be made as strong a place as any in the world with a little charge, and so there is a retiring place, for the fearfull that have thoughts of departing the Kingdome; it were not amisse to call all that are gone thither; and let them pay excise there towards our war rather than the wars of others.

Let all who apprehend the gaining this Towne a good piece of service to the State, give the noble Earle of Manchester his due praise, and God the glory.

This is Licensed, and Entered into the Hall Booke according to Order.

Printed by G. *Bishop*, and R. *White*.

⁂ Notes ⁂

p. 1 **'Fortifying it selfe under pretence of Neutrality'** —
During the early months of the war many people clung to the
hope of peace and postponed as long as possible taking any steps
which committed them irrevocably to either side. In Lynn,
however, the situation seems rather to have been that a faction
in control of the Common Council supported Parliament, but
that during the spring and summer of 1643, it gradually lost
ground to royalist supporters in the town, strengthened and
organised by gentry from the surrounding countryside.

p. 1 **'The Earle of Manchester'** — Edward Mountague, Earl
of (God)Manchester, was appointed Major General of the Eastern Association (Essex, Cambridgeshire, Suffolk, Norfolk,
Hertfordshire and Huntingdonshire) in succession to the un-
satisfactory Lord Grey of Wark, in August 1643. He was the
single peer whose arrest was unsuccessfully attempted by the
King at the same time as the Five Members.

p. 1 **'for the freeing of Lincolneshire'** — After the capture
of Gainsborough by the Earl of Newcastle's royalist army in
early August, 1643, the county of Lincolnshire was almost
completely over-run by the King's supporters.

p. 1 **'Old Lyn'** — now known as West Lynn, was then a small
hamlet on the west bank of the Ouse. See p.7.

p. 1 **'Granadoes'** — mortar shells.

p. 1 **'the Causey that leads to the South'** — was the Setchey
road leading out from the South gate. The road to Gaywood
led out from the East gate.

p. 2 **'fired two houses in Gauwood'** — According to Mason
(History of Norfolk, 1884) this was achieved by a small force

sallying out from the East gate. Two houses and the Hospital, or Alms house, were destroyed and ten townsmen were killed in the skirmish.

p. 2 **'pioneers'** — were employed as labourers by the army's engineers; they were considered below the rank of ordinary soldiers.

p. 2 **'halfe Musket shot'** — the maximum range of a musket was between 200 and 300 yards.

p. 2 **'a drake bullet'** — a drake was a medium-sized cannon, also known as a 'saker'.

p. 3 **'The Commissioners for my Lord Manchester'** — Sir John Pagrave (Palgrave) of North Barningham, one of the new baronets created in 1641 in a belated attempt to recruit support and revenue for the King, was nonetheless an active supporter of Parliament, and led a somewhat disorderly contingent of the Norfolk militia as a Deputy-Lieutenant. He was a member of the Norfolk Committee and at one stage was accused of being 'very timidous' (R. W. Ketton-Cremer 'Norfolk in the Civil War' 1969 p. 198). He was certainly a moderate, but remained active in the Parliamentarian cause and distinguished himself at the siege of Newark. He was elected knight of the shire in 1647. Colonel Francis Russell, of Chippenham Hall in Cambridgeshire, was the officer in charge of the entry into Lynn. He was a personal friend and comrade of Cromwell's and his daughter Elizabeth married Cromwell's son, Henry, in 1653. Philip Calthrop (Calthorpe) of Gressenhall was possibly a relation of James Calthorpe of East Barsham who was appointed Colonel in the militia in place of the royalist Sir Nicholas Lestrange. A Robert Calthorpe was a member of the Common Council of Lynn. Gregory Gosset (Gawsell) of Watlington was on the

Norfolk Committee and one of the Commissioners for Sequestrations, also a treasurer of the Eastern Association. He was
High Sheriff of Norfolk in 1649. John Spelman of Narborough
was the stepson of Sir John Potts of Mannington, a leading
Norfolk Committee man. He was an ardent Parliamentarian
and quite out of sympathy with his royalist kinsman Sir John
Spelman who was in arms for the King.

Colonel Valentine Walton (Wauton) had married Cromwell's sister Margaret in 1617. His home and estates were at
Great Staughton in Huntingdonshire. Early in the war he had
acted with Cromwell to prevent the plate of the Cambridge
colleges from being sent to the King. He was taken prisoner
at Edgehill, but was later exchanged for the royalist Sir Thomas
Lunsford. His wife Margaret died at Lynn in 1644 and his son,
Valentine, was killed at Marston Moor in July 1644 when he
received from Cromwell the famous letter beginning, 'Sir, God
hath taken away your son by a cannonshot...'. (See Antonia
Fraser, 'Cromwell; Our Chief of Men', 1973, p. 129.)

p. 4 **'Those for the Towne'** — Supporting Sir Hamon Lestrange (see Introduction) were Captain Robert Clench, a captain of the Lynn Town Bands, Sir Richard Hovill of Hillington,
Thomas Hudson, Mayor-elect, and the complete legal establishment of Lynn, Francis Pallet (Parlett), the Recorder, William Leeke, the Town Clerk, and Walter Kerbio (Kirby), an
attorney. Master Dearing or Dearham remains obscure.

p. 4 **'a Common-Hall'** — a meeting of the Common Council
of Lynn in the Trinity Guildhall.

p. 4 **'Delinquencie or Malignancie'** — The King's supporters
were called 'delinquents' or 'malignants', not 'royalists' in the
early stages of the war, since the Parliamentarians maintained

the convenient fiction that they were fighting for 'King and Parliament'. (See the Earl of Manchester's medal on p.3)

p. 5 **'the 400000 pounds'** — This sum is somewhat mysterious, but perhaps represents the national total Parliament intended to raise from all counties by the 'weekly assessments'. Norfolk was supposed to contribute £1250 per week, of which Lynn's share was £27 11s. 9d. The Hall books show that the town had raised £525 15s. 6d of its arrears and that through the efforts of Toll and Percival Parliament had agreed to allow £400 of this money to be retained to pay for the fortification of the town.

p. 5 **'Delinquents sent for by the Parliament'** — In May, 1643, Parliament had ordered the apprehension of Sir Hamon Lestrange, his sons Nicholas and Roger, his relative Sir Charles Mordaunt of Massingham, and a number of other royalist gentlemen. They were to be disarmed and sent to Wisbech gaol.

p. 5 **'Members of the House of Commons'** — John Percival and Thomas Toll, M.P.s for the town, were put under house arrest during the royalist coup. Toll, whose house backed on to the Ouse, later escaped by jumping into the river and swimming or rowing to safety.

p. 5 **'the Association'** — The Eastern Association was formed in April 1643 as a means of raising a unified Parliamentarian army from the counties of Essex, Suffolk, Norfolk, Cambridgeshire and Hertfordshire. Huntingdonshire joined soon after and Lincolnshire later still. It was hoped thereby to keep the fighting out of these counties.

p. 8 **'the Earle of Warwick'** — Robert Rich, Earl of Warwick, was the Lord Lieutenant of Norfolk appointed by Parliament in 1642 to replace Thomas Howard, Earl of Arundel and his son, Lord Mowbray. He was largely responsible for bringing the navy into the war on Parliament's side and spent most of the war at sea. During the weeks of the siege of Lynn, he blockaded the port and prevented supplies being brought in to the defenders of the town. One royalist vessel escaped his ships by giving false signals.

p. 9 'vindication of the Mayor' — It is not at all clear whether the two mayors covering this period, Thomas Gurlin (1642-3) and Edmund Hudson (1643-4), were active royalists or whether they were tools in the hands of the royalist gentry. Gurlin was much absent from Council meetings during his year as mayor, and died the following year, so may have been in poor health. Attempts by Sir Hamon Lestrange to exonerate Hudson were not successful. When John Perceval died in 1644, the freemen of Lynn tried to elect Hudson as their M.P., only to find that he was still a marked man. He was disqualified from sitting for 'having assisted at the rising of Lynn'. (Hillen, 'History of King's Lynn', Vol. I p. 343).

p. 12 'not many fighters' — Apart from the rebellions of 1549, there had been no real fighting in England between the reign of Henry VII and the outbreak of the Civil War. Military experience could only be gained on the Continent or in Ireland. The Trained Bands (local militia) were supposed to exercise monthly, but their military skills were not very highly rated.

p. 13 'Captain Rich' — possibly Robert Rich, grandson of the Earl of Warwick, who later married Cromwell's daughter, Frances. He was on the Norfolk Committee and had served under Cromwell at the capture of a nest of royalists at Lowestoft in March, 1643.

p. 13 'lately lockt up' — This refers to his imprisonment at

Oxford after Edgehill.

p. 14 **'Master Ash'** — The Revd Simeon Ashe, one of the chaplains of the Earl of Manchester. Ketton-Cremer suggests that he may have been the author of this pamphlet.

p. 14 **'Entered into the Hall Book'** — There is in fact no sign that the whole pamphlet was copied into the Book, but the terms relating to payment of Manchester's army were written in — in very small writing!

Norfolk Museums Service, King's Lynn Museum.

The East Gate of Lynn, from an engraving of 1741.

After the Siege

The siege of King's Lynn lasted three weeks and, according to the pamphleteer's estimate, involved the loss of 'above eighty lives'. (The parish registers are not helpful in proving or disproving this number.) On any military scale it was a minor operation, but its importance was great, both for the town and for Norfolk. Effectively the surrender of Lynn kept the eastern counties clear of military operations for the duration of the first Civil War, although the towns and villages were to be reservoirs of troops and supplies for the Parliamentarian armies. For Lynn itself the whole episode was a disaster. It became a garrison town for the duration of the war, with all the financial and social burdens that such status involved. The sum of £2,300 had to be raised from the town immediately to pay the occupying army and its officers, and the payment of the garrison during the remaining years of the war would have been a pressing necessity, the ravages of unpaid troops being a more immediate danger than any attack from the royalists.

Considerable damage was done in and around Lynn during the weeks of the siege. The Lestrange accounts mention houses destroyed near the South Gate, William Johnson's mill burned down, haystacks burned, the destruction of the Hospital at Gaywood and the bridge at Setchey. The west window of St. Margaret's was severely damaged and, from the evidence of an eighteenth-century engraving, so was the East Gate. No doubt there was other indiscriminate damage done by the 'granadoes' lobbed into the town by the Parliamentarian mortars. For the greater part of this damage Sir Hamon Lestrange was held to be responsible, though

Mayor Gurlin's heirs and Captain Clench are also mentioned as contributing to compensation. Sir Hamon was allowed to retire to his home at Hunstanton and the spirit in which he paid damages to Lynn and its new governors is clearly reflected in his wife's account books:

'Payd to May, Wormell etc. for their
pretended losses   225 li 11s 2d
To Mr. Percivall for pretended imprisoning   86 li'

She claimed they had been plundered in 1643 of 1600 sheep, all their corn and divers horses, and estimated that they paid £1088 over a period of six years 'by the unjust and tiranicall oppression of Mr. Toll and others of his faction in Linne'. Small wonder that the Lestranges felt a sense of injustice when Toll and Percival, together with Colonel Walton, were appointed assessors of their own damages.

Political divisions within the town clearly did not end with the Parliamentarian victory. Some members of the council whose covert royalism had been revealed by the events of that autumn quietly withdrew from their civic duties. Parlett, Leake and Kirby were discharged 'at their own request' in December 1643, and Thomas Dix and John Barritt followed in January 1644. The 'Gentlemen strangers', who had been the natural leaders of Lynn's revolt, departed, leaving the town in the hands of those acceptable to Colonel Walton. Once Lynn was felt to be safe, Walton appointed an acting governor, Colonel Hobart, whilst he was busy in the capital where he had his own splendid establishment at Whitehall.

The King and his supporters, however, continued to harbour hopes of support from Lynn. Charles I gave an ill-considered commission to young Sir Roger Lestrange to foment further trouble in the town in 1644, but this only led to his capture and imprisonment for four years in Newgate gaol under sentence of death. When the defeated King finally abandoned Oxford in 1646, he travelled briefly into Norfolk with a few of his personal friends in the faint, but futile, hope that Lynn might provide support or an escape route. Sir Hamon Lestrange came under suspicion again in both these years, but, whatever his sons might involve themselves in, he remained politically inactive. He died in 1653, being visited on his deathbed, at some personal risk, by his son Roger, and it is fair to say that, despite all the begrudged payments to Lynn and to the Commission for Sequestrations, there was still a considerable estate to divide between his sons. Lady Lestrange died in 1656.

Finally, at the Restoration in 1660, the tables were turned once more and it was the turn of the other side to suffer. Colonel Walton had participated in the trial of Charles I and his signature was on the death certificate; he was therefore excluded from the Act of Indemnity. Leaving his second wife behind in England, he made haste to the Continent, where he became a burgess of Hanau in Germany. According to rumour he finished his days in the Low Countries earning his living as a gardener. Hillen, however found evidence of him living in good society in Dordrecht and possibly working for the Dutch secret service. He died in 1664.

Chief Sources

Primary Sources
Lestrange family accounts — Norfolk Record Office
The Hall Books — King's Lynn Borough Archives

Secondary Sources
Hillen, H. 'History of the Borough of King's Lynn' 1907
Ketton-Cremer, R. W., 'Norfolk in the Civil War' 1969
Kitchin, George, 'Sir Roger Lestrange' 1913
Mason, R. H., 'History of Norfolk' 1884
Parker, V., 'The Making of King's Lynn' 1971
Richards, P. 'King's Lynn' 1990
Richards, W., 'The History of King's Lynn' 1812